# dear free lanc er

by Brittany Melton

To my Mom and Dad who taught me to be a leader, to feed people with a long-handled spoon, and to always leave my lights on if I'm not home.

BE NOT
WEARY IN
WELL-DOING
FOR IN
DUE SEASON
YOU SHALL
*reap*

## An Introduction

In 2014, I came home reeling from a divorce. My finances were in shambles, my pride crushed, and my self-worth non-existent. Unfortunately, bills don't care you're going through an emotional death.

I was so broke. I was having to choose between a working cell phone and health insurance. There were times I had to let my bank account stay negative so I could use the cash  I had to pay for gas to see a local client. It only took a few weeks for me to start drowning in debt. Something had to give.

After fumbling my way through many online courses, and quite a few harshly learned experiences, I figured enough out to find a sustainable source of clients.

It was hard. It was messy. I started from the bottom and I am no where near the top. What I have learned is that you don't need a bunch of specialized knowledge to position yourself properly. You just need someone to help you through the ups and downs that are common to every freelance industry.

This book is my attempt to keep you from struggling the way I have in the past. This is my attempt to be that someone that pulls you along when the journey is too much.

DEAR FREELANCER, SOMETIMES YOU WILL HAVE TO TAKE A DETOUR TO GET TO YOUR FINAL *destination*

There is nothing like living from paycheck to paycheck when you have big goals for your freelance business.

You finally reach a moment where you can breathe and start to consider putting some money in your long-neglected savings account. Even your bank account is negative a lot less than it used to be.

Then, one client decides to skip out on their final payment and your whole life is ruined. You are desperate to pay your bills on time and get back to the balance you knew for what seemed like one pay period.

Now you have a choice: quit, or find another client, probably in a niche you hate.

It is okay. We have all been here. Go ahead, swallow your pride, and send that pitch.

DEAR
FREELANCER,
DESPITE WHAT
REJECTION IS
TELLING YOU,
YOU ARE MEANT
FOR THIS *life*

It was a shoo-in, right?

They sent you email after email about how they cannot wait to work with you. You got so hyped, sent the invoice, and then crickets.

After a week or two, you finally get a follow-up response with some apology and some excuse about rates. You are heartbroken. And then, you are angry you wasted your time getting your hopes up.

It happens.

And this will not be the last time this happens.

Clients come and go. There will always be another, more worthy client worth pitching.

Get back in the game and start pitching. A better opportunity is waiting.

DEAR
FREELANCER,
NOT EVERY
ASPECT OF
FREELANCING IS
*fun*

It is so easy to start a new project and believe that you have created your dream job. Then your pipeline starts to dry up and you have to hit the Internet pavement to market yourself.

Or, you finish job after job without correctly sending invoices and suddenly it is tax time.

Or, even better, you get a credit card chargeback because a client decides they want to use their non-refundable deposit to pay a cheaper Freelancer.

Now, you have to dig up the half-completed contracts you created and figure out how to affordably hire an attorney.

This is freelancing.

It is not always glamorous. Often, it is the boring, or tedious, tasks that have the most significant return.

Stop procrastinating and get back to work. Keep going. Eventually, you will be able to hire an underling to deal with all of these shenanigans haha.

DEAR
FREELANCER,
IF YOU ARE
WORKING ALL
THE TIME YOU
WILL *burn out*

It wasn't your intention to live paycheck to pay-check. But, somehow, despite receiving deposits for five jobs back to back, this is where you have landed. And, if you don't work, you don't get the final payment.

You're trapped.

You over-committed because the numbers for your ideal workload didn't add up to bill payments.
There is no time to get any sleep. Who has time to cook? Let's order takeout. Hobbies? Never knew her. Ain't no time.

Keep telling yourself this and watch how sick you get shortly after. Watch how long you stay sick. And watch how many balls you drop.

Go. Get some sleep.

DEAR
FREELANCER,
IF YOU NEVER
TRY YOU WILL
ALWAYS BE *rejected*

Portfolio Shyness is a serious epidemic.

There will never be a time when you are proud of your portfolio. Either it is extremely out-dated, ugly, or sparce. Maybe all three.

But, you are your worst critic every time. The interesting truth is that most clients have no idea what a bad portfolio looks like. Most clients hire you because they like you, your enthusiasm, or style.

So put yourself out there, crusty portfolio and all. Your portfolio is not as bad as you think.

DEAR FREELANCER, PUBLISH THAT POST THAT HAS BEEN SITTING IN *drafts*

You are in the shower and you finally figure it out. The piece of content that will change the game for your freelance funnel. You hop out, grab a towel, and get to writing. Then return to the rest of your work because bills gotta get paid and you have deadlines.

The next day comes and you read what you wrote. You hate it. So, you work on another content idea that came up. The cycle repeats.

So now, a month later, you have released no content and you have twenty-six drafts in WordPress. Your conscience is getting to you because you know consistency is key. So you pick a random one and publish it.

It gets hundreds of shares and hundreds of views. You're a hero. You are getting follow-up tweets thanking you for sharing what they desperately wanted to see.

Maybe done *is* better than perfect.

DEAR FREELANCER, COPYING YOUR COMPETITOR MAKES YOU THEIR *shadow*

You are on Twitter minding your business and a tweet rolls by that catches your eye. You click the link and OMG look at this website.

Now you hate everything you have ever created and you want that. That one they have. Everything else is canceled, in the name of Jesus.

But maybe, just maybe, you liked that site because you are their target audience. Your audience is not theirs. Your audience is yours. And your audience loves your site. How do you know? Your analytics show you the views and shares you are getting on your work.

I mean, unless you are self-conscious about your brand. But maybe it is time to ask yourself if you are willing to drop everything and jump to a new design, is your brand missing the mark?

DEAR
FREELANCER,
DON'T AVOID
CONFLICT
BECAUSE IT
MAKES YOU
*uncomfortable*

The customer is always right. Until... they are violating their contract. OMG.

Now you're at a crossroads. You have to be mean and enforce your policies, charge that fee, or close that project. But what if they put your brand on blast on social media? How will you go on? How will you find new customers? How will your reputation survive?

But, if you allow one customer to punk you, what is to stop them from referring their friends with identical behavior? And, maybe you are uncomfortable because you are supposed to be speaking up. And maybe, just maybe, that discomfort is there to prompt you that this situation is whack.

Get going.

Respect the discomfort.

Enforce your policies.

DEAR FREELANCER, MOST YES'S ARE REALLY *no's*

"I love your work."
"Let me think on it and get back to you."
"I'd love to collab".
"Let's connect sometime. I love what you're doing."
18K Retweets. 46K Likes.

If none of these "good things" includes a contract and deposit payment, it is a no. Until actual money is exchanged, do not assign business value to these things. You will save yourself so much stress.

# DEAR FREELANCER, STICK TO YOUR *policies*

No one expects people to show up, pay, and then screw them over.

But it is always the least suspecting people who do.

The one with the ridiculous turnaround time request, but who is unwilling to pay a rush fee. Or the one who skips the final payment so they can hire someone else to finish your work---that's theft by the way. Or the one who balks at your asking price and asks for a discount for the culture.

Stick to your policies. You will *always* regret making the exception.

DEAR
FREELANCER,
FEAR MEANS
WHAT YOU ARE
CREATING IS
*needed*

You hear it all the time. The market is oversaturated. We don't need one more product in that category.

However, if you have noticed a problem with the products that exist and no one is solving it. Go for it.

The fear you're feeling is the fear associated with being different. Being different is how brands are built and distinguished from their competition.

Besides, it doesn't matter how many makeup brands appear, we always find money to support a new one. Why can't that same principle apply to you?

DEAR
FREELANCER,
NO STRATEGY
WILL MAKE THE
HARD WORK
ANY LESS *hard*

There is nothing like the excitement of starting a new project. You are so hyped in the newness of it all. So you sit down to figure out how to make the thing happen, after all, you have announced it to your timeline.

Oh my gosh it's going to take longer than you thought.

Maybe there is a quicker way to get started.

Down the rabbit hole, you go. Hours later, you don't find the shortcut you need, and now you're discouraged.

In all the time you spent looking for a shortcut, you could've been halfway through the longer, more detailed route by now. Get to work. Everyone starts at the beginning.

DEAR
FREELANCER,
IT MAY
TAKE YEARS
TO GET YOUR

*footing*

The Internet has a way of making things take three days. Or at least, that is how it seems. Three days to get a thousand newsletter subscribers. Three days to your first viral marketing campaign. Three days to a million page views. Three days to your first $10,000.

All of those promises are probably true. But, the only people they are right for are those who have previous experience. Those who aren't starting from near zero.

You, however, need to put in the time to pay your dues---like ordinary people. Anyone that tells you otherwise is selling you lies. Bottom line.

DEAR
FREELANCER,
LIKES,
RETWEETS,
OR SHARES,
ARE NOT
*purchases*

On the Internet, success is never success until it goes viral. Then suddenly we are validated. Suddenly we feel comfortable to promote ourselves. Suddenly our ideas are making waves.

However, with virality, only a few people will click your link, and read your post. Or buy your product.

You could get that same amount of people from focusing on authentic marketing. Small shares, but high clicks and sales is always a win. That is how marketing works.

DEAR
FREELANCER,
IT IS OKAY
TO BE NEW
AND TO MAKE
*mistakes*

These days no one wants to be new. Because all of the actual experts are telling new people you need to be an expert to position yourself to sell.

Let me tell you that many people will pay to learn as you learn. I know this from experience.

Do not get caught up in the trap of claiming expertise on things you have learned from other people. You lack the experience to back that expertise up. And, you lack the experience to evolve those ideas further.

It is okay to be new. You can and will make money now. Your newness will not scare your ideal audience away. Plenty of people are out there who are okay with hiring beginners. That is how we all got started, after all.

Get to work.

DEAR
FREELANCER,
STOP OBSESSING
ABOUT HOW TO
MAKE IT ~~AND~~ *create it*

Research has its place.

You should always make sure your content title isn't taken and that your URL is available. And yes, if you have no idea how to use that software, you should spend a few minutes watching tutorials.

But there is only so much information you can absorb without executing what you have learned. The best way to learn and get results that help motivate you to continue is to execute as you learn.

It is time to get started. The longer you wait, the more coins you are leaving on the table.

DEAR
FREELANCER,
IF YOU NEVER
MAKE TIME FOR
IT, IT WILL NOT
*get done*

It is so easy to go from project to project, hoping to make enough in deposits to pay your bills. Your actual content, which is key to building your brand and authority, gets put on the backburner in favor of finishing client work and finally getting those final payments.

You will look up from this cycle, usually around the time your leads run dry and your bills are overdue, and wish you had been consistent with your newsletter, blog, or product creation.

Break the cycle now.

Spend some time, even just an hour, on your projects. On projects that will make you money without a client's approval.

You will thank me later.

DEAR
FREELANCER,
DON'T LET
DISCOMFORT
KEEP YOU FROM
PAYING THE *bills*

"My audience is too small."
"I don't want to be a spammer."
"I am not one of those pushy salespeople."
"I feel awkward promoting."
"I have never promoted to my audience, wouldn't it be awkward if I started now?"

Every Freelancer enters this spiral.

Your audience, however, gave you their email address, followed you, or subscribed to your blog, because they are interested in you and what you do. So promote yourself. Right now. Put this book done.

DEAR
FREELANCER,
YOU WILL NEVER
MAKE A LIVING
WAGE IF YOU
DON'T ASK

*for it*

There is nothing like the first lead you get after you raise your prices. Did they see your old prices? Are they going to pay these higher rates?

Deep down you know you raised your prices because you absolutely cannot survive with the clients and money you have now. But these new prices feel extremely high. What should you do?

Let me tell you, you will *always* regret undercutting your current prices. Not only are clients problematic when you low-ball yourself, but you will begrudingly work through the whole project thinking you deserve more for your work.

DEAR
FREELANCER,
KEEP GOING
IT GETS *better*

It will always get better.

With time, you learn how to market more efficiently. With time, you learn how to pitch better. With time, you learn how to deal with difficult clients with confidence.

But those things always come after the slow times, the hard times, and the frustrating times.

Don't give up.

DEAR
FREELANCER,
RAISE YOUR
RATES. YOU
*deserve*

I was in a coffee shop working, as I often am, and I heard a business owner bragging about her new hire.

The hire was a freelancer who had an excellent portfolio, excellent work ethic, and excellent customer service. But the reason the owner chose that Freelancer over others was because they charged significantly less than what they were worth. She called it a steal.

She said she would have hired them even at a higher rate but she knew they were naive about pricing and had to take advantage.

Long story short, you are playing yourself by undercharging. Business owners know, and can afford, to hire you at the right rates. Raise your prices.

DEAR
FREELANCER,
YOUR EXPERTISE
IS *valuable*

It always starts with a simple question.

"How did you get started?"

That question turns into a full interview and next thing you know you have spent hours coaching someone for free.

Even better, you wait a few days and they are charging other people for the knowledge you gave them.

Do not give away for expertise for free. Ever.

DEAR
FREELANCER,
YOU CANNOT
"PULL AS YOU
CLIMB" IF YOU
CANNOT PAY
YOUR *bills*

There is nothing like the feeling of putting together a community of freelancers who look like you and want the thing you want. Suddenly the loneliness dissipates and it becomes so much easier to make it through the sludge of freelancing.

But the worst feeling is devoting countless hours to the community only for them to never improve and never grow. Especially, since those countless hours have taken away from the hours you need to make money to pay bills.

The lesson?

Rebalance and recenter. Devote the countless hours to yourself and your bills. Give the spare hours in between to others.

DEAR
FREELANCER,
EXPOSURE
RARELY LEADS
TO A CONSISTENT
SOURCE OF
*clients*

No matter who it is, no one can guarantee that exposure will bring you the clients you need to pay the bills. Even more, the exposure that might land you a client, won't come before your upcoming bills are due.

You are worth being paid for your labor. Working without payment is illegal. And at the end of the day, you can't tell the power company you will pay them in exposure.

As hard as it may be, that means that you will have to stop saying yes to writing for that community blog four times a month. And you will probably have to stop saying yes to being a guest on that Twitter chat that conflicts with your self-care hours.

DEAR
FREELANCER,
AN INQUIRY IS
NOT A
RESERVATION.
RESERVATIONS
ARE MADE WITH
*cash*

"I would love to work with you."

This was said to me by a writer, and community organizer, I adored online. I loved her style and her brand. And, I could not wait to be a part of the brand team.

After a few emails back and forth, I gave her a discounted price for work and sent the invoice.

Crickets.

Followed up and received a few responses back and forth. Then sent a reminder email to her, after being assured she would work with me.

Crickets.

After a few weeks, I followed up one last time to receive a response like I thought we could do more of a collaboration instead of a paid project.

Womp womp womp. Joke's on me. And I missed bills that month because of ....collaboration.

DEAR
FREELANCER,
IN ALL THINGS,
YOU GOTTA
PAY YOUR *dues*

"Be an expert in your field."

This is the poor advice given to new freelancers and business owners in niches they have no experience in. So instead of taking some time to learn a discipline, to do the work, and gain some experience, people pretend to be an expert.

And to pretend, they steal the advice of actual experts. Steal as in learn directly from that expert, then parrot the advice without giving credit.

That is a horrible way to start your business. And it is a surefire way to make an unsustainable business. By the time you have the expertise, no one wants to work with you.

DEAR
FREELANCER,
REST IN THE
FACT THAT
YOUR LANE IS
EXCELLENT AND
*timely*

Nothing like starting a new thing, and seeing some-one who started at the same time as you, kill it with an easy to copy idea. I could do that.

So you deviate. And start doing that.

And that becomes a lot more cumbersome to do. And suddenly, you've wasted months, or even years, chasing an idea that should have been easy to do.

And let me tell you, there is nothing like the sinking feeling that comes when you realize you wasted time you could've spent on the original, *amazing* idea you abandoned.

Spoiler Alert: that's how *Dear Freelancer* started and stopped.

DEAR FREELANCER, THERE'S A REASON YOU CLOSED THAT DOOR. DON'T OPEN IT *again*

Everyone has it. The worst client ever.

The client who requests 50-11 revisions but doesn't want to pay for them. Then doesn't respond promptly, but is angry at the delayed timeline. Then they don't pay on time. And then they do a chargeback so they can hire someone else with the money.

Womp womp womp.

It is always this client that is on the timeline requesting more work. Willing to pay. And at a time you really need the money.

There is a reason you just processed that refund even though you weren't wrong. leave that door closed, hun.

DEAR
FREELANCER,
YOU HAVE ALL
THE TOOLS YOU
NEED ~~TO GET~~ *started*

I know you want to know exactly what tool your fave used to get the photos they produce. Or maybe you want to know what website platform they used to build the site you are jealously staring at.

But, at the end of the day, you have one of two options, hire a professional to get what they have, or spend countless hours teaching yourself hoping that your two-digit bank account can get you four-digit results.

That is not how any of this works.

It is okay to use the starter tools. It is okay to use the free option. Do whatever it takes to get started and get going. The money will come when it is time.

DEAR
FREELANCER,
APPLY FOR
WORK
*regulary*

I am going to be so painfully honest. I *still* struggle with this lesson.

There is nothing like the hype of booking out to make you conveniently forget to fill your social media scheduler that week.

And there is nothing like having your bills paid on time for the first time in months to make you neglect your newsletter. But, even though those wins didn't come quickly, they can be quickly snatched away.

One client refund. One late payment. And, everything is ruined.

Ask me how I know.

DEAR
FREELANCER,
MAKE SURE
YOU BUILD
YOUR OWN
HOME BEFORE
YOU BUILD FOR
*others*

There are a lot of excuses we tell ourselves when we write for free, or offer free services, to community organizations.

I am giving back.
I am pulling up as I climb.
I want to see them grow.
I want to help the community.

There is nothing like the feeling of seeing a community owner monetize a platform, and fail to pay the people doing the heavy lifting. And even worse, nothing like the feeling of seeing a community owner shut the platform down, or change niches, and remove your hard work.

If you neglect your website, your own digital home, you are not protected when things like this happen. You lose everything. It is okay to help communities grow, but please protect yourself first.

DEAR
FREELANCER,
INDECISIVENESS
IS KEEPING YOU
FROM BEING *paid*

You don't need anyone's permission to start, stop, or change things involving your brand.

In fact, the more you ask for permission the more you are allowing other people to dictate a vision to you that is contrary to what you have in mind. The moment others start sounding off doubt gains a foothold.

Content topics. Product ideas. Brand collateral. You, not your audience, should decide all of these things.

And let me tell you, every decision I have made alone, from wearing unicorn hats to posting pokemon gifs has allowed me to create a brand that is unique and recognizable---you know how brands are supposed to be.

DEAR
FREELANCER,
GET ONE
INCOME STREAM
PROFITABLE
BEFORE JUMPING
TO *another*

It is so hard.

Admitting that you have no idea what to do next with your business.

It is usually at this point that you chicken out and switch to another great, but completely unestab-lished, idea. But a marvelous thing happens when we stop and get honest with what you want, and why.

Usually out of that comes your next step. Often the truth is it is so far out of our comfort zone that we lie and claim we don't know what to do.

You know what must be done.

Take a deep breath and get to work. You can do it.

DEAR
FREELANCER,
SETUP SOME
DEADLINES FOR
YOUR PERSONAL
*goals*

It is one thing to say you want to make six figures in five years. It is an entirely different thing to say you want to make six figures by September 1st, five years from now.

On the surface, those two seem the same. However, when you add a date to a goal, it becomes real. Usually not real when we are five, four, and three years out. But, when we start closing in the realness hits and we start taking tangible action.

I used to think this was terrible. If I could just spend five years working on a five-year goal I would knock it out the park.

But, I believe the most significant lessons are learned in the trash that we throw against the wall in the first few years, in an attempt to figure things out. Getting the trash out of our system, and learning from the experience, allow us to monopolize the last one to two years.

DEAR
FREELANCER,
WHEN THINGS
GET HARD JUST
FOCUS ON
THE NEXT *Step*

It is wise to set goals with deadlines.

However, sometimes we become so obsessed with the deadline that we overwhelm ourselves trying to get there.

Step back.
Take a break.
And figure out what the next step is.

By focusing on next steps you will likely take a route that is better than the largely estimated route you planned initially.

DEAR
FREELANCER,
MOST PEOPLE
COMPETING WITH
YOU, GIVE UP
*quickly*

Most people who copy, steal, and cheat give up so quickly.

The time you spend invested in what others are doing is time that is taken away from your growth and trajectory.

The truth is that they cannot take away your views, experiences, and personality. So even if they lift an idea, or are creating something similar to what you want to create, it won't end the same way. That is your advantage.

So when you find yourself focusing on others and wondering where your progress is, step away. Go create something and come back. They'll be on something new in three months, often even less.

DEAR
FREELANCER,
IT IS OKAY
TO ADMIT
YOU'VE *failed*

There is a big difference between failure and lack of patience.

For quite some time I would abandon ideas before they got appropriate traction out of lack of patience.

The hard truth is almost nothing gains traction immediately. Unless your audience has been prepared months before, almost nothing you put out there will sustain itself immediately. Ignoring this fact, and quitting regualrly, hurts your enthusiasm, motivation, and ego.

Make it a point to stick with something for at least six months before you give up. Some things are a super flop this doesn't mean you failed, it means you missed a piece of the puzzle. Take some time to explore this, before you quit.

DEAR
FREELANCER,
TEST YOUR IDEAS
TO SEE IF THEY
ARE WORTH.
*pursuing*

Spend a quarter secretly launching a product.

Put it out there, work out the kinks, and build a list. Don't make a big deal of it, just test it to see if people naturally want it.

Then the next quarter properly launch it using a new name, or a new package. This way you don't start from zero, you get results immediately, and your ego stays intact through the process.

DEAR
FREELANCER,
A FINISHED
PIECE OF ART IS
ALWAYS BETTER
THAN ONE THAT
IS PERFECT BUT
*unfinished*

Producing subpar work sucks.

You know what I mean. The work that turns out completely different than you thought and not a good kind of different.

However, in actually finishing you got to learn the entire process start to finish. So now, the next time you create something similar, you know how to improve every aspect of creation.

If you keep quitting too soon, becuse something is not perfect, you will never learn how to complete projects. Even worse, you will have no idea how to manage your energy so your enthusiasm survives from start to finish.

DEAR
FREELANCER,
THE TIME YOU
SPEND MAKING
THINGS PERFECT
IS ALWAYS TIME
*wasted*

This is a hard lesson I am still learning.

With every product I design for my client, there is always that list of things I would like to improve before I send it for revisions.

But the hard truth is that my level of expertise is so far above theirs. That's why they hired me. So they likely don't notice the fifty-eleven things I think are wrong.

Finding a balance between good enough, and perfect is so tricky. But if your time is worth a lot of money, and it is, you save money to sooner you accept that good enough is preferred.

DEAR
FREELANCER,
UNDERSTAND
THAT YOU CAN
HUSTLE ONLY IF
YOU ARE *healthy*

Hustle Culture will tell you that it is normal and expected to work all day and all night on your side hustle.You won't make it if you don't put in the hours immediately.

These things, on the surface, are correct. But, if you are sacrificing your health to put in the hours, you are hustling backward. If you are skipping meals to work on client work you are playing yourself.

The truth is that your clients understand that you cannot be available all day and all night. They aren't after all. Your clients will understand that that extra round of revisions isn't free. Teach them.

You can't hustle if you're sick, and exhausted.

DEAR
FREELANCER,
A SKILLSET PAYS
THE BILLS NOW.
EXPERIENCE
KEEPS THE BILLS
PAID *consistently*

Can't just buy an expert level item and think you'll win. You can't just do what your neighbor is doing and think you know best now. No, you have to *learn* your path.

What you ignore when you focus on buying expertise is that every person has a unique upbringing, skill-set, and set of experiences that make their expertise *their* expertise.

I can't even count the number of times I bought a product not realizing the amount of time it would take me to get that five-minute tutorial video correct. I can't even begin to explain the money I have spent thinking I would get the same ninety-day results despite my living situation is entirely different.

It isn't the product that makes you an expert, it's you. And if you haven't put in the time you aren't an expert yet. And that is okay.

People will still pay you.

DEAR
FREELANCER,
TOOLS ARE
USELESS IF YOU
DON'T HAVE THE
*skill*

I've been designing for over a decade at this point. So yes, I can show up with a free tool and make it look expertly designed. It is not the tool that is important, it is the skill.

Once you do something so many times you know precisely what to look for to get the results you want. But the key is you have to do something *so many* times. If you have only done it once, twice, or even ten times, you have a while to go.

Go get started.

DEAR
FREELANCER,
YOUR TIME IS
INTENSELY
*valuable*

I get asked a lot about whether people should switch from website platform X to website platform Y because Y has a feature X doesn't, and the need it.

You don't need that feature, nine times out of ten. What you need is to either hire a professional to do the switch, so you save time, or sit down. The time you spend fumbling through setting up a new platform is time taken away from growing your list, advertising your next product, and onboarding a new client.

And, if you are being honest, the only reason you are questioning what you are doing is because you feel inadequate compared to someone else. Or, you feel like you need a certain tool, or certain look, to be taken seriously.

Do not let pride have you out here wasting your time, especially if what you are doing is working.

DEAR
FREELANCER,
DON'T LET
HYPE CONVINCE
YOU TO SET
UNREASONABLE
*goals*

I know it hurts so bad to admit it. But if you haven't made a thousand dollars yet, you aren't going to know how to make ten thousand, or more. If you haven't done what it takes to grow your audience to a hundred subscribers, you aren't going to magically have a thousand in any arbitrary amount of time.

Instead of hoping and guessing, set reasonable goals based on where you are now.

I know, that means you have to throw out your plan for the year because it is based on unknowns and a *lot* of random guesses. But isn't it better to succeed *incrementally* than to spend month after month continually failing?

Start small. Small goals add up quicker than you think.

# DEAR FREELANCER, FEAR DOES NOT GO *away*

It is okay to be afraid.
It is okay to not be okay.
It is okay to feel feelings that are often associated with negativity.

Those things don't go away. And honestly, who would you be if they did?

Once you recognize these feelings and face them, you start to recognize the lies they're telling you. And more and more you start to recognize those lies faster.

So yeah, as you push past your comfort zone you are going to hear voices that push back and tell you this is dangerous. By the way, those voices are your natural sense of flight trying to protect you. Recognize them, and push through anyway.

Every opportunity you really want is on the other side of fear.

# DEAR FREELANCER, RAISE YOUR *rates*

The amount of money you make does not define you. However, if you are freelancing, certain clients appear at certain price points.

If you can offer higher caliber work, as you can as you get more and more experience, you should raise your prices.

You deserve to work with people who know the cost of their time and thus are willing to pay you appropriately.

You deserve to work with people who have hired freelancers before and thus know it is unacceptable to get free revisions, or out of business hour work.

Raise your rates.

DEAR FREELANCER, YOU DON'T HAVE TO WORK FOR A CELEBRITY TO BE VALID OR *profitable*

Here is a truth you need to grapple with.

Why do you want to work for insert famous company here? Why do you want to be seen in insert famous magazine here?

Sure, some opportunities will come your way if you are smart enough to be ready for them. But the harsh truth is that more often than not, major companies and celebrities expect free, or low paying labor. That is how they turn a profit. And they expect this labor to be high-caliber labor, often with a very small turnaround time.

Unless you are sitting on savings, do not put your bank account stability at risk chasing fame. Chase coins instead.

DEAR
FREELANCER,
STOP GIVING
YOUR BEST
WORK TO
OTHERS IN
EXCHANGE FOR
*exposure*

In theory, everything we produce will be our best, or be produced at a level high enough to be considered good. But often that isn't the case. And often, it is the work we create for communities we deeply care about that happens to be our best.

If you are creating good work, maybe it is time to place that content, product, or service on your website instead of letting someone else own it.

Maybe it is time to put yourself, and your own financial stability, ahead of non-paid opportunities. And maybe it is time to have faith in yourself enough to know people will pay you for the work you have been giving away for free.

DEAR
FREELANCER,
STOP QUITTING
BECAUSE YOU
ARE AFRAID OF
*success*

On the surface, this is a strange statement.

Why would anyone be afraid of succeeding? Of course, you wait because you didn't want to fail. Right?

But what happens if you succeed?

What happens when more people know you?

Are they going to attack you and your character?

Are they going to dig up some part of your past you're trying to hide?

Are you going to suddenly be more accountable than you want?

These are questions we ask ourselves when ideas start to get traction. And they expose part of ourselves that we need to work on.

DEAR
FREELANCER,
YOU CANNOT
DUPLICATE THE
SUCCESS OF
*others*

Whenever I see someone who started when I did and is crushing it in a lane I feel like I could perform in I have to myself, why do I want to do what they did anyway? Why do you want to be the next insert name here? Why do you want to be the black version of in-sert name here? Why are you selling yourself short?

You are telling yourself you want to be a copy of someone else because you covet what they have.

No.

Instead, of working to be the next so and so, sit down and figure out what makes you happy and how you want to succeed. You will find competition to be less of an issue then.

DEAR
FREELANCER,
MOVING AT A
SLOWER PACE
DOESN'T MAKE
YOUR PROGRESS
ANY LESS *valuable*

Life happens.

And contrary to what Hustle Culture will imply, you cannot physically maintain a rushed pace indefinitely.

So when life happens, and you are forced to slow down, maybe due to illness or disability, it is okay.

Progress is progress, no matter how fast it comes.

DEAR
FREELANCER,
YOU NEVER
FINISH YOUR
TO-DO LIST
BECAUSE IT IS
ALWAYS TOO
*long*

It isn't until life happens that we usually realize how far behind we are on specific goals and tasks.

For example, the moment you get sick is the moment you are stressed out by your to-do list. If you find yourself in this position, clear your list.

Yes, I'm serious. Throw the whole thing away.

Grab a new sheet of paper and add one to three things to it. Work on those before adding anything else.

I know that is so hard when you are behind on everything. But you only have so many hours and overwhelm and anxiety can quickly steal too many.

It is time you get honest with yourself about what you can and cannot do.

DEAR
FREELANCER,
SOCIAL MEDIA
SHOULD NOT BE
YOUR ONLY
SOURCE OF
*income*

At the beginning of 2018, so many freelancers got kicked off of their biggest platform because new spam rules changed. There are even people I have been following for years who are now being censored.

While censorship can happen anywhere, and at any time, it is so difficult for it to happen in your own home. If you have neglected your website or your newsletter, take some time to create a content plan you can stick to and get back to supporting yourself first, before you support others.

At the end of the day, these online platforms are businesses.

They put themselves over others because they have money to make. And it is time you start doing that too.

DEAR
FREELANCER,
YOU CAN BE
AFRAID OF YOUR
NUMBERS, JUST
REVIEW THEM
*anyway*

You cannot improve if you don't know where you are now.

If you are making any financial goals or audience based goals, you have to know where you are starting from. I know, if it has been a minute since you looked at your analytics it is scary. What if your numbers are zero?

But you cannot improve without knowing.

And the sooner you find out, the sooner you can correct your course. You can do it. Put the book down and look at your metric right now.

DEAR
FREELANCER,
YOU NEED A FEW
PEOPLE IN YOUR
LIFE THAT WILL
LISTEN TO YOU
*complain*

This book, and my entire career, would be nothing without the three people that have been there to listen and relate to my gripes and complaints. So I want to end this book with a reminder that you cannot make it out here alone.

No one is self-made, and that is okay.

You learn to succeed much faster when you have people encouraging you, walking with you, and laughing at the shenanigans for you.

Don't go at it alone, even if that means that you need to reach out to people you met on Instagram.

DEAR
FREELANCER,
LOVED THIS
BOOK BUT NEED
SOME HELP AND
*support!*

If you enjoyed this book, there is a companion course available that will walk you through the mindset mistakes we, as freelancers, often make when setting our prices, raising our prices, putting ourselves out there, and create new products and service.

If that sounds like something you desperately need, hop on over to the Dear Freelancer website to get started. The course is just a week long and comes with worksheets, videos, and emails to get you through.

Sign up for the 7-Day course at dearfreelancer.co/course

## About the Author

Brittany Melton has been freelancing for over ten years in the field of Web Design and Development. She has a bachelors of Science in Software Engineering and spends most of her day neck deep in WordPress code. When she isn't freelancing, she is cracking jokes on Twitter @xobritdear.

Made in the USA
Middletown, DE
20 July 2019